I ENCOURAGED ME

65 THOUGHTS TO TAKE YOUR CONFIDENCE TO THE NEXT LEVEL

SHARNETTE BERRIE

EVYDANI BOOKS

I Encouraged Me

IEncouragedMe@gmail.com

Unless otherwise identified, Scripture quotations are taken from the **King James Version.**

Scripture quotations marked **BSB** are taken from the **Berean Study Bible.**

Scripture quotations marked **ESV** are taken from the **English Standard Version.**

Scripture quotations marked **KJV** are taken from the **King James Version.**

Scripture quotations marked **MSG** are taken from the **Message Translation.**

Scripture quotations marked **NASB** are taken from the **New American Standard Bible.**

Scripture quotations marked **NIV** are taken from the **New International Version.**

Scripture quotations marked **NKJV** are taken from the **New King James Version.**

Scripture quotations marked **NLT** are taken from the **New Living Translation.**

Scripture quotations marked **VOICE** are taken from the **The Voice Bible Translation.**

Publication & Interior Layout: EvyDani Books, LLC

Cover Design: LKB Designs & Photography

Editing: Nzadi Amistad Editing and Writing Services

ISBN: 978-1-7361534-2-0 (paperback)

Printed in the United States of America

In memory of my loving sister,
Sharene Lynette Beasley
March 6, 1969 – September 25, 2018

INTRODUCTION

I Encouraged Me was written after I learned how to keep myself encouraged. It wasn't always easy to turn to anyone, especially when I was being physically and mentally abused.

When the mental abuse started, I confided in someone who was close to me. How many people know that, sometimes, the closest ones to you are the ones who will try to destroy you? Well, this was the case for me. I was shut out from the outside world and had to deal with the mental abuse that turned into physical abuse.

Through the tears, I thought, How could God allow me to go through this when He said that He would protect me? I can remember, one day, I was sitting on the couch with a knife, begging God to make it all stop. I wondered, How can I go on suffering in silence when it will only cause me more harm? Do I continue to pray, or do I finally try to reach out to someone who can help me get past the mental abuse once the physical abuse has stopped?

One afternoon, while I was sitting in my room, I turned on a tape by Shirley Caesar that I had received from my grandmother. As the song began to play, I looked up and said, "God, if I can just encourage myself, then I know that I will be able to help others who are suffering from the same thing."

So here I am now, finally putting together this book to encourage you through me.

PRAY THROUGH EVERY SEASON

"Pray without ceasing."
1 Thessalonians 5:17 (KJV)

Stay on top of prayer at all times. Even if things are going well, you must continue to cover yourself at all times. Things will not always be 100 percent, as some things will occur that are beyond what you can fix.

Always remember that, when you pray, you need to have enough faith in God that you can leave it alone. Your prayer will carry you to a different level of trust so that you can move forward.

WHEN TRUST BECOMES AN ISSUE

"He is not afraid of bad news; his
heart is firm, trusting in the
Lord." Psalm 112:7 (ESV)

*O*ftentimes, we find ourselves looking for the right person to trust. Most of us have been through some things that we couldn't find a way to talk to anyone about. We did things that we weren't proud of and, also, have trusted some people within our crew, telling our darkest secrets, when we should have taken it to our graves.

This is when we should put our entire trust in God. It's safe, and one thing about it, you won't hear it again, but you sure will get confirmation regarding it.

FEELING GUILTY

"If we confess our sins, he is
   faithful and just to forgive us
   our sins to cleanse us from all
   unrighteousness." 1 John
   1:9 (ESV)

One must admit when guilt has played a role in their life. Whether it was something you said or did to someone known or unknown, it may still be heavy on your mind. It's not easy to move forward from guilt. It will have you staying on stuck mode because, every time you think that you are moving forward, that guilt will creep back and say, "I'm still here."

Don't let the guilt of what you should've done hold you back from moving forward. Make peace, pray, and carry on. You have the right to eliminate guilt. Confess whatever is making you feel shame, guilt and regret.

THINGS THAT I USED TO TRIP AND STUMBLE OVER, I NOW WALK OVER.

"My enemies have trampled upon
me all day long. For they are
many who fight proudly against
me." Psalm 56:2 (NASB)

*L*earn how to walk over the trap that was set to take you down. You have to know that, when the trap is set in front of you, it is meant to harm you. You may trip. You may stumble or lose your balance as you try to grip the situation, but you won't fall. Look at the traps as if they are mazes and work yourself out of them.

Walk over it. Make that left. Walk straight. Make that right. Continue straight, and you're almost at the end of the maze...the exit from your existing problem (stumbling block) is in front of you.

WHAT DO YOU DO WHEN GOD PROMISES YOU PEACE AND YOU GET CHAOS?

"I sought the Lord, and he
answered me and delivered me
from all my fears." Psalm
34:4 (ESV)

This is the time when you will need to shut completely down, get into a private place, and go before God. There's a reason why chaos has now temporarily risen above the promise. When you prayed over the things that were shattering your life, God was bringing peace your way. When you saw things beginning to change, you went backward, to the very same thing that God was separating you away from.

Sometimes, God will allow this to happen to show you that your recovery needed to be revoked until further notice. However, don't faint in the chaos. God has never left a promise unfulfilled.

YOUR REST IS GOING TO COME
FROM GOD

*"Come unto me, all ye that labour and are heavy laden,
and I will give you rest."*
Matthew 11:28 (KJV)

We've all, at some point, heard the phrase "I'm sick and tired of being sick and tired," right? This is the point where nothing seems to be working out in your favor and you are just fatigued after going through everything with no wins. This is when you will find out that, after all the turning back and forth, sleepless nights, calling on friends, turning to things that may make you comfortable for just a moment, you're right back in that sinking space.

Seek God for all your needs, and then you can rest. All your rest will come from Him after you turn over to

Him every situation that has been causing you to be uneasy.

KNOW WHEN TO WALK AWAY

"Walk away from the company of
    fools ... It takes wisdom for the
    clever to understand the path
    they are on." Proverbs 14:7-8
    (VOICE)

*D*on't stay stuck in any situation when you
have the option to walk away. Don't hold
on to things that don't make you stronger. People will
suck the life out of you and leave you drained, to the
point where you feel that the only way for you to move
forward is by being around them. Not so, you can move
on and leave them right where they think they left you.

No love lost. You just gained your strength back.

THEY EXPECT YOU TO FALL (FAIL)

> "I am the Lord, the God of all mankind. Is anything too hard for me?" Jeremiah 32:27 (New International Version [NIV])

Why wouldn't they? After all, you knew that it was time to start a new chapter that didn't include them. They've seen you mature. They've seen your growth, and then they found out that separating yourself from them would have you in line for that miracle that you have been waiting on.

Now, since the miracle has gone into effect, they don't know how or why things have begun to look more positive on your behalf. They want to know how you are doing this without them. They expected you to fail because they thought that you needed them to survive.

DON'T LET YOUR EMOTIONS CAUSE YOU TO TURN AROUND

"Search me, O God, and know my heart: try me, and know my thoughts…" Psalm 139:23 (KJV)

Our emotions can get the best of us at times, especially if the problems that we are facing involve the loss of a job, trouble in our home, family issues, or death. These incidents can force negative behaviors or emotions to go into overdrive.

We tend to let that light trigger on with emotion to match the situation. It's okay to act on your emotions if you are not able to control them. Just don't let your emotions cause you to turn away from the growth that changed you.

THROUGH THE HARD TIMES...I DIDN'T FOLD

"You know that under pressure,
your faith life is forced into the
open and shows its true colors."
James 1:3 (MSG)

*J*f you don't have the correct resources to help you get through tough times, you will feel as though you are under pressure, and it will become a struggle because, once you hit that low level, then you will be too embarrassed to seek help from family or friends.

However, behind-the-scenes situations taught me how to not fold, and because I didn't fold, I pulled through.

THERE IS A SOLUTION FOR YOUR PROBLEM

"There is the confidence we have in approaching God: that if we ask anything according to his will, he hears us." 1 John 5:14 (NIV)

There is a solution to every problem. Prayer. Pray with confidence and without ceasing believing that God will hear you.

PRAY-Morning

PRAY-Noon

PRAY-Night

WORK YOURSELF THROUGH THE PROCESS

"But as for you, be strong and do
not give up, for your work will
be rewarded." 2 Chronicles
15:7 (NIV)

Sometimes, you might hit a low point in life, not because of you doing something wrong, but because God is about to do something big in your life, and there is nothing that anyone can do about it but watch. Your low point will be shifted around.

Keep pushing and working through the process. The progress is coming along good.

GOD MADE ME WHO I AM

"But by the grace of God I am what
I am, and his grace to me was
not without effect." 1
Corinthians 15:10 (NIV)

*P*eople will give you an identify based off someone else's opinion of you. If that person recruited others, then all of them together will come against you with lies and rumors. And they will make assumptions about you.

One thing that is for sure is that God will always show someone who you are through Him. Your walk and talk will outweigh any rumor or lie. He will shut the mouths of your doubters.

YOUR BLESSING WILL OUTWEIGH
YOUR BURDENS

"For our light affliction, which is
but for a moment, is working
for us a far more exceeding and
eternal weight of glory ..." 2
Corinthians 4:17 (New King
James Version [NKJV])

*A*lways remember, you will have things that
will weigh you down to the point where you
want to know where God is in all of this. We all have
some things that can be similar, and other situations
can be something that others have yet to face.

Hang in there. Once the blessings start to hit, you will forget about what you went through.

I CAN FORGIVE; HOWEVER, ALL THINGS DON'T NEED TO BE REPAIRED

"Get rid of all bitterness, rage and
anger, brawling and slander,
along with every form of
malice." Ephesians 4:31 (NIV)

*I*t wasn't easy for me to forgive a person that did me wrong. The lies and backstabbing had me in a place where, every time I heard that person's name, thought of that person, or even saw that person, it would put me in a place of wanting to retaliate. I wanted to do them the same way they had done me.

Then, it clicked. I was damaging myself by not forgiving that person, and I couldn't grow into the next stage of life if I didn't forgive. Although things can't be repaired, forgive yourself and live.

YOUR HAPPINESS SHOULD MEAN MORE TO YOU THAN NOT BEING DISAPPOINTED

"For the Scripture says, 'Whoever believes in him will not be disappointed.'" Romans 10:11 (WEB)

*Y*ou can only get or be disappointed with yourself when you have relied on a person that wasn't dependable. Others can only disappoint you when they have the power over you to do so. You were happy before it occurred, knowing that you had to trust God, who has a record of never disappointing man.

Therefore, keep your happiness by not seeking things from others. Your happiness depends on your belief in God.

"Practice these things, immerse
   yourself in them, so that all may
   see your progress." 1 Timothy
   4:15 (ESV)

on't let anyone or anything stop you from
going to the next level.

That problem-GROW

That lost friendship-GROW

That heartache-GROW

That loneliness-GROW

That disappointment-GROW

Pain caused by others-GROW

LEARN HOW TO BE YOUR OWN BEST FRIEND

"Do not be misled: 'Bad company corrupts good character.'" 1 Corinthians 15:33 (NIV)

Certain situations will have you not wanting to talk to anyone but God. You may have even experienced unwanted situations that made you want to separate from others. All company is not good company. Once you accept the fact that you may have to be your own best friend, you will understand that you can go and have fun alone.

REST IN GOD'S RESPONSE

"Come to me, all you who are
weary and burdened, and I will
give you rest." Matthew
11:28 (NIV)

You will get responses from people just wanting to hear your business. At times, you may believe that they are there for you, so you might lean on their shoulder or use their ear to listen, so you can vent. You don't want their opinion all the time, knowing that they wouldn't take their own advice all the time; therefore, their feedback isn't wanted.

However, God's response is the only perfect response that you can get. He is already there and is waiting on you to come to Him. Pray your way through and wait. His response is just a prayer away, and you will receive the answer through confirmation.

YOUR DECISION DOESN'T CHANGE YOUR PROMISE

> "Have I not commanded you? Be
> strong and courageous. Do not
> be afraid, do not be
> discouraged, for the LORD your
> God will be with you wherever
> you go." Joshua 1:9 (NIV)

We, sometimes, make decisions according to how we feel. Some decisions could be for the best, and others could be something that we shouldn't have done. I, basically, mean that we went in the wrong direction. We did it our way because of a lack of patience, because we didn't trust God during that season.

One of the many things that I love about God is that He never holds it against us when we feel as though we can do it without Him. Nope. He will simply watch it unfold. When you feel that you need Him, all you have to do is step back, let Him take over, and watch Him do what He does. Your decision did not change His promise. He still worked it out.

GO THROUGH BEING UNCOMFORTABLE. IT WILL MOVE YOU TO GET OUT OF THAT SITUATION

"So do not fear, for I am with you;
do not be dismayed, for I am
your God. I will strengthen you
and help you; I will uphold you
with my righteous right hand."
Isaiah 41:10 (NIV)

Uncomfortable situations often make us want to throw in the towel. We think that we are supposed to have this perfect life where nothing bad is supposed to happen. God will use us as examples to show others (unbelievers) how He brought us out. They will trust Him after seeing our strength and faith.

God will purposely put us through that situation because we have been too comfortable. If He was to let us be comfortable at all times, we would not need His direction to bring us out of that uncomfortable state of mind.

> "For I know the plans I have for
> you," declares the Lord, "plans
> to prosper you and not to harm
> you, plans to give you hope and
> a future." Jeremiah 29:11 (NIV)

*I*t's going to happen according to God's plan. One thing we must keep in mind is that, what we think is good for us, God will delay it or take it away if He knows that it will be of harm to us. His elimination of something that will harm you, instead of help you, will show you how much you can rely on Him to have your back. What you don't see is God's way of saying "NO."

Therefore, you may not see it right now but just know that God is working behind the scenes on your behalf.

PROTECT YOUR PEACE

"Deceit is in the heart of those who
plot evil, but those who
promote peace have joy."
Proverbs 12:20 (NIV)

*J*ust a reminder: You do not have to draw yourself into someone else's mess. Their mess might cause you to have side effects that will eventually affect you. For example, it can have you taking on the problems of others that have nothing to do with you. You might begin to feel angry because of conversations you have had regarding someone else, or they will drag you into someone else's battle, drama, etc.

Protect your peace at all costs. Keep a level mindset by knowing that your peace comes before anyone's mess.

LOVE IS LIFE AND LIFE IS LIVING

"We know how much God loves us,
and we have put our trust in his
love. God is love, and all who
live in love live in God, and God
lives in them." 1 John
4:16 (NLT)

*L*ove is a powerful word. Life is what you live, and living it is what's important. In order for you to love someone, you must first love and then fall in love with yourself. We must realize that, once we love ourselves the way that God loves us, then we will be able to love someone else and live.

Show that same love that God is showing us on a daily basis, and then you will learn how to live life with love.

YOUR HAPPINESS SHOULD MEAN
EVERYTHING

"Those who listen to instruction
will prosper; those who trust
the LORD will be joyful."
Proverbs 16:20 (NLT)

*B*eing happy should be a part of your day-to-day lifestyle. You are responsible for getting to a place where you can think of something old or new that will put a smile on your face just because.

The legendary Melba Moore blessed me with her Seven Commandments of Melba Moore to live by:

1. Stay away from negative people

2. Focus on your own life
3. Stop trying to keep up with the Joneses
4. Stay out of your own head
5. Never live beyond your means
6. Pray daily and remain positive
7. Stop seeking others' approval

Your happiness matters!

LIFE IS ABOUT THE JOURNEY, NOT THE DESTINATION.

"For he will command his angels
concerning you to guard you in
all your ways." Psalm
91:11 (NIV)

Oftentimes, life can take you on an unexpected detour. Things may have run their course in your life, and these things may have forced some of these changes. You may feel that you have been fighting each destination that you have arrived at but always remember: "Life is about the journey." It may have ups and downs; however, the journey will make memories that will outweigh the length of the destination.

Always remember, as you journey on, that God is with you.

DON'T BE AFRAID OF CHANGE.
GROW IN IT.

"He will never leave you nor
   forsake you. Do not be afraid;
   do not be discouraged."
Deuteronomy 31:8 (NIV)

*C*hange is good. Don't get stuck in the same habit that will cause you to be at a standstill when you should be moving forward. When you face the same habit over and over again, you should be focused on what you can do to get to another level without being afraid to go. When you see yourself moving toward greatness, you will be able to look back and see the change, knowing that you left the fear behind.

Always know that you can grow to your next level. It will look good on you.

HOLD ON. DON'T QUIT... GOD IS ON YOUR SIDE

"Now faith is the assurance of things hoped for, the conviction of things not seen." Hebrews 11:1 (ESV)

Don't let the absence of an immediate answer from God cause you to doubt or resent Him. Instead, let it be an occasion to deepen your faith. Hold on a little while longer. God is answering prayers and performing miracles on a daily basis.

Keep the faith.

I'M NOT PERFECT BUT GOD IS

"For all have sinned and fall short
of the glory of God." Romans
3:23 (NIV)

$\mathcal{D}$on't consider yourself the type of person that has to be perfect at everything. I have to remind myself of that. When something goes wrong, it's ok. Things happen, problems occur, disappointments take place, but as long as you give it your all, that is all that matters. None of us are perfect, but we serve a perfect God.

Therefore, know that it is ok when something unexpected happens.

CORRECTION SHOULD MAKE YOU BETTER, NOT BITTER

"Watch out that no poisonous root
of bitterness grows up to
trouble you..." Hebrews
12:15 (NLT)

J had to learn this as I sat in church one Sunday morning (the fourth Sunday of 2010) as my godfather, Bishop Dozier C. Shields, was preaching. It made me think (in a zone), Wow! It's ok not to be right all the time. I learned through his sermon that being corrected is how you learn from a mistake of thinking that you were right. That taught me how to be better, not bitter.

Know that it is ok to be corrected. It will give you the opportunity to help someone else to better themselves through you.

IF YOU NEED TO CRY...CRY

"He will wipe away every tear from
their eyes..." Revelation
21:4 (ESV)

*L*et your tears flow. Don't hold them back. We all get to the point where we have been strong in front of people for so long that behind closed doors is when the tears flow. Some tears flow heavier on different days, but we continue to hide them with a smile.

It's ok to let others see your tears. The reason for your tears could possibly help someone who has been needing to let theirs out, too. You never know how you could affect someone else through your tears.

YOUR NEXT STEP

"Though I walk in the midst of
trouble, you preserve my life."
Psalm 138:7 (NIV)

Your next step should be your best step. While you are going through your trials, you may face different obstacles that will make you feel like you should quit. Don't let the trouble that may come your way make you go back to that place that is now unfamiliar.

Tell yourself, "Self, this is not the time to stop. There is no reason to quit or take steps backward!" Remind yourself that your next step will be your best step.

IT'S NEVER TOO LATE

"Whether you turn to the right or
the left, your ears will hear a
voice behind you, saying, 'This
is the way; walk in it.'" Isaiah
30:21 (NIV)

No, you didn't do it years ago. You'd rather take a detour to do other things. Maybe it was to have fun. Maybe it was a career path or just simply giving your time to help others. Whatever it was, it's never too late to start fresh.

If you don't pray… START praying! Now is the time to start connecting to God through prayer.

Go back to school. Don't let what it costs stop you from fulfilling your life goal.

Use what you have to accomplish your goal. Someone you don't know is rooting for you!

NO RESONSE IS A GOOD RESPONSE!

"Don't respond to the stupidity of a
fool." Proverbs 26:4 (MSG)

There will be times when you will have to
"shut yourself up," instead of responding.
Remind yourself that some people don't deserve
feedback, especially regarding things that do not
concern you.

They may try to push it on you; however, you shouldn't
waste your time trying to please them. There is no need
to explain yourself. Just shut them down with silence,
and then tell your silence, "Thank you. Job well done."

IT WASN'T THEM... IT WAS YOU/ME

"Lots of people claim to be loyal
and loving, but where on earth
can you find one?" Proverbs
20:6 (MSG)

*B*laming someone for something that you could've handled is just another excuse for you not owning up to what you allow to continue. You did it because you thought, for the thousandth time, that person would change. You thought for the five-hundredth time that person would be by your side as you have been for them every day. You thought for the one-hundredth time that their loyalty would match yours when you know that you're one of a kind. Your loyalty is rare.

It wasn't them that kept coming back to you. It was you. You were scared that you would miss out on their life of nothing. Let that go. You owe yourself more than what you have been given. It's ok to add to self.

YOU CAN MAKE IT PAST THE PAIN
AND THE HURT

"The Lord is close to the brokenhearted and saves those who are crushed in the spirit." Psalm 34:18 (NIV)

Yes, it hurts. Yes, it costs you great pain. No, you were expecting that situation to unfold. How could someone do that to you? It wasn't supposed to happen like that. Sometimes, you just have to say, "Okay. It did happen," and know that God brought you through that hurt that caused an uncomfortable pain, and you survived it.

ROAD TO SUCCESS

"And I will make them and the
places round about my hill a
blessing…" Ezekiel 34:26 (KJV)

The road to success isn't a straight shot. There's a curve called failure, a loop called confusion, speed bumps called friends, cautions lights called family, and you will have dead ends called jobs, but if you have a spare called determination, an engine called perseverance, insurance called faith, and a driver called God, then you will make it to that successful place.

Keep avoiding all distractions. Success is in your view.

LEAVE IT BEHIND YOU

"If the Lord had not been on our
side when people attacked us."
Psalm 124:2 (NIV)

orget those things which are behind you
(holding you back) and press forward to
the things that serve your purpose in life to finish
strong. You are covered to move forward, and with
God's help, you will not fail. Old friends may try to
remind you of your past, and they may try to entice you
to go back or try to attack you, but the way that God
has your life set up, you will be able to say, "If it had not
been for the Lord who was on my side."

Your strength and ability will push you in the right direction. Look ahead with a smile.

WE HIDE DEPRESSION WELL

"But you, Lord, are a shield around
me, my glory, the One who
lifted my head high." Psalm
3:3 (NIV)

*D*epression is not easy to deal with, especially
when you feel as though people will look at
you differently. It often takes you into a sunken place
while you're trying your best to keep a smile on your
face so that others won't know. That alone feeling will
have you feeling lonely in a room filled with people.

I had to look depression in its face and declare that it
wouldn't take control of me any longer. The little bit of

strength that I had left and my love for my daughter were enough for me to fight with faith. Depression used to be one of my struggles, but I overcame it with the will to fight.

TEARS HIT DIFFERENT WHEN YOU'RE PRAYING

"Give thanks to the Lord, for he is
good; his love endures forever."
1 Chronicles 16:34 (NIV)

Oftentimes, when I pray, I find myself talking to God, and as soon as I say the words "thank you," I find myself getting teary eyed. I've often thought, Why is this happening from those two words more than others? Then, it came to me, after all that God has done for me on a daily basis, when I thank Him, it's a sensitive moment for me. The reason for this is, out of all the bad things I've done, He's kept me going and has never held it against me.

I'm very grateful that I can count on God at all times, and you should be grateful, too, because you are reading this knowing that God has blessed you, too.

PROCRASTINATION IS A DELAY TO YOUR NEXT LEVEL.

"Don't put it off; do it now! Don't rest until you do."
Proverbs 6:4 (NLT)

I've put things off because I wasn't sure they would play out as planned. For example, I've put off writing this short book. As I was writing, I spoke to three different individuals that I trusted. Each one gave me their best answers, but then a fourth person, who I hadn't spoken to in a while, appeared. She was sent by God. After I asked her for advice, she said, "Don't wait no longer. We are waiting for this to happen. Don't ask no more questions to anyone else. If you need to stop, ask God, and let Him lead you. Finish it and get ready to help others through you."

I now say, "Don't stop right there." Someone is in need of help that only you can give. God gave us talents that can push someone ahead. Don't delay another moment. Get that talent together and go forth with it.

MY BOUNCE BACK IS DIFFERENT

"Therefore, if anyone is in Christ, he is a new creation. The old has passed away; behold, the new has come." 2 Corinthians 5:17 (ESV)

I had to move forward from being stuck to the same things that I was accustomed to. I had to let go of some things that I thought that God had for me when it was me that thought that it was good for me. I had to walk away from situations that I wanted to hang on to. I wanted to retaliate against my emotions, but I fought back. I began to move different because I wanted different, and that was when the change began.

My strength that I applied came from me going into prayer and asking God to change me. I gave it all to Him and watched how he started to handle things right before my eyes. It was because of my prayers that my bounce back became my weapon.

TRUST GOD FOR A SUDDEN SHIFT

"He has perfect timing: never early,
never late. God is never in a
hurry, but He is always on time."
- Anonymous

Feelings will take control when things seem out of control. It will feel like you are going in circles, running into a brick wall, on the edge of a mountain, or your frustration level has hit an all-time high.

At any given time, God will show up. He will give you a sudden shift, shake that feeling around, and show you that He can be in one hundred different places but will always be on time at every location.

Trust Him in advance.

TALK TO YOURSELF

"Thank you for making me so
wonderfully complex! Your
workmanship is marvelous—
how well I know it." Psalm
139:14 (NLT)

*I*t's okay to talk to yourself, as long as you're
saying something good!

Tell yourself, "Good morning."

Tell yourself, "I'm BEAUTIFUL."

Tell yourself, "I'm GREAT."

Tell yourself, "It's just a TEST."

Tell yourself, "I can DO IT."

Tell yourself, "I'm closer than I was YESTERDAY."

Tell yourself, "I can MAKE IT."

Don't wait for someone to tell you these things... validate yourself. God told you that you are because of Him.

LETTING GO

"He says, 'Be still, and know that I
am God.'" Psalm 46:10 (NLT)

I became stronger once I let go of the very
things that were holding me back. I took a
look, and it seemed that I was in the same place I was a
year ago when I said, "This is definitely my year. There
will come a time when you will need to be still, observe
the things around you, and then see the bigger picture,
in order for you to strive to your next accomplishment.
It will take you to let go. This may be the time where
you have to walk alone. Depend on God more to get
where you need to go.

REBUILD TO PROTECT

"Again, I will build you, and you
will be rebuilt!" Jeremiah
31:4 (BSB)

ebuilding yourself to accomplish more
than what you have lost is a top priority.
Everyone isn't meant to be there; therefore, that could
be one of the many reasons that God had to take it
away from you. You didn't get completely wiped out.
God just shifted around some people and some things
to get you back on track. While they watched, God was
preparing you to rebuild.

Rebuild using what God has left you with. Follow the direction that He is taking you in and let His protection carry you forward.

YOUR FUTURE DOESN'T CONSIST OF THE PAST

"'With man this is impossible, but
with God all things are
possible.'" Matthew 19:26 (NIV)

Bad experiences have made some of us believe that we are cursed. We believe that what we went through in the past was something that reoccurred over and over again due to making the same mistake that was dealt to us because of our family background. It's ok to break that curse that could've been passed down by previous generations. Make sure you look at yourself in the mirror and say, "Whatever happened in my past will not affect my future. Yes, I made mistakes. Yes, I was incarcerated. Yes, I did the things that people are talking about, but most of all, I changed, and my past will no longer hold me hostage."

Because of God, I was able to turn this situation around. Take a look at me now.

ONCE YOU RESPECT YOURSELF, OTHERS WILL FOLLOW SUIT

"Be strong and courageous. Do not
be afraid or terrified because of
them, for the Lord your God
goes with you..." Deuteronomy
31:6 (NIV)

There are so many people to want to fit in.
People do whatever they have to in order to
seek clout for a come up. At times, fitting in will cause
you to do things that are not normal. Some will dress in
ways to get attention but will get labeled as something
that they are not. Someone will have you act on a
reaction that has nothing to do with you. Your name
will ring bells, according to how you carry yourself.

Don't be afraid to let your respect for yourself be shown.

Don't be fooled by someone foolish when you can be wise by respecting yourself. Be courageous in all that you do. Your respect for yourself will go further than you can imagine. A wise person is a person that a foolish person will follow.

ONE OF THE MANY REASONS WHY I LOVE HIM… HE NEVER FAILED ME

"Jesus Christ is the same yesterday, today, and forever." Hebrews 13:8 (NKJV)

In all ways, we should appreciate God for the many things He has done. Family and friends may let us down, but GOD has never failed us. He does more for us on a daily basis than we can do for ourselves.

GOD IS:

A Healer – doctor that's always on call

A Keeper – when we thought we couldn't be kept

A Provider - our needs will get met

A Protector – from all hurt, harm, and danger

A Shelter – keeping us safe in the midst of any storm

God will never change!

APOLOGIZE. THERE'S NO "BUT" IN BETWEEN

"Pride goeth before destruction,
and an haughty spirit before a
fall." Proverbs 16:18 (KJV)

People's pride will kick in when it comes to apologizing, knowing that they are wrong about a situation. This could lead to people not speaking to one another and/or relationships being destroyed. Pride will take people in directions that could've been avoided if only an apology was made without justifying it with a "but."

Don't let pride and a "but" make you lose a good relationship. God forgives us every day as we should forgive others.

HURT TO HEALED

"Heal me, o Lord, and I shall be
healed." Jeremiah 17:14 (KJV)

hen you have no other choice but to learn from the hurt that someone else has caused you, that is when you will realize that you can live through it to start the next process. God has a way of building us back up from that low point of hurt. It is not always easy to bounce back from a situation, especially when you were done wrong by someone who you looked up to. However, God will take the broken pieces and put them back together again, but He will leave out the piece that did the most damage and replace it with something better.

Don't sit there and hurt when the process of your healing can start.

WHEN THEIR WORDS DON'T ADD UP

"It is better to take refuge in the
Lord than to trust in man."
Psalm 118:8 (ESV)

$\mathcal{Y}$ou'll meet (so-called) good people who will say, "Trust me. My word is bond. Don't fold on me, and I promise I will not fold on you," but they will turn around and show you the opposite. This will leave you thinking, Who can I trust? Those people are the ones that you have to be very careful with. Always pay attention to their actions. They will never lie...their words do.

Their words could never add up to what they can and will show you.

REMIND YOURSELF THAT YOU ARE GOOD ENOUGH

"The LORD will accomplish what
concerns me; Your
lovingkindness, O LORD, is
everlasting; Do not abandon the
works of Your hands." Psalm
138:8 (NASB)

*D*on't continue to put yourself down... lift
yourself up. What are you waiting for? You
have the ability to make yourself feel good. Just because
you have been down doesn't mean you have to stay
there. Put on that suit or dress. Add the necessities to
go along with it. Put on that smile as you look in the

mirror, and tell yourself, "I am good enough, and from this day forward, I will live as if it is my last day."

With God on your side, you can accomplish things in life without waiting for anyone to give you the green light.

KNOW WHEN TO PUT YOU ON MUTE

"One who guards his mouth and
his tongue, Guards his soul
from troubles." Proverbs 21:23
(NASB)

There will come a time when you will have a
lot to say, but God will shut you up when
nothing needs to be said on your behalf. Know when to
let God address the necessary things that involve you,
instead of feeding into a conversation that involves
others. You have a choice. Decide what to entertain and
what to eliminate from your life. I've learned that

putting myself on mute keeps me from being connected to the wrong people, places, and things that mean me no good.

You can and will become a wise person when you learn how to let God use you on mute.

DON'T BE SAD THAT IT'S OVER

"Some trust in chariots and some in
horses, but we trust in the name
of the Lord our God." Psalm
20:7 (NIV)

S ome things happen quicker than others. One minute everything seems ok, and the next minute, things take a turn. There will come a time when you think that you need someone in your life, and suddenly God removes them without warning. Then, you have the things that last longer in someone else's life, which make you wonder, Am I doing something wrong? The way that God is set up, He will wreck a situation before He lets it harm you. Trust His process.

Know when to accept what GOD is doing and praise Him for it. He makes no mistakes and know that what He does is for your good. Don't be sad that it's over. Be happy because it happened.

NEVER GO SO FAST THAT YOU FORGET TO VIEW YOUR PROGRESS

"Thanks be to God for his
indescribable gift!" 2
Corinthians 9:15 (NIV)

*D*r. Marquis Boone posted the following message on his Instagram page: "We can clearly see how far we have come but can miss the message of how far we came." It's always good to reflect and see our progress, for we know that we have come a long way. You have been on this journey that has taught you real life situations and skills that got you where you are today. Today you have shown yourself that what God gave you was a gift, and you are walking in it.

Slow down, look back, and then thank God for the victory.

EVEN ON A BAD DAY, YOU HAVE TO SEE HOW FORTUNATE YOU ARE

"Then you will call on me and
come and pray to me, and I will
listen to you." Jeremiah
29:12 (NIV)

You won't see that bright light every day, that light that beams down while you're looking up with a smile. There will be days when things will not go as planned because of what happened the day before, because it is still lingering around in your mind. You try to move forward with your day, but you keep letting that nagging moment play games with you; therefore, you can't function. You can get back to the smile, if you can let go of yesterday today. What happened then shouldn't affect your now.

Say a silent prayer knowing that God is listening.

YOUR PLAN VS GOD'S PLAN

> "'For I know the plans I have for
> you,' declares the Lord, 'plans to
> prosper you and not harm you,
> plans to give you hope and a
> future." Jeremiah 29:11 (NIV)

I have to remind myself that, although it seems like things are not going according to plan, God's plan is better. We have to realize that whatever we plan is just that. If it is not lined up with what God has for us, it will never work. Don't be discouraged because you should prefer for it to be a plan of success, instead of a plan that will fail. When you are least expecting it, a shift of excitement will overcome you. That is God showing you something better.

You are now on the wave that God ordained to take you to your next phase. Get ready to level up.

THE STRONG ONES HAVE WEAK MOMENTS

"Therefore encourage one another
and build one another up, just
as you are doing." 1
Thessalonians 5:11 (ESV)

*A*n encourager will pick up a phone, answer text messages, or meet someone that is going through a rough moment. We love to help out people in any way we can. It's not often when the encourager gets encouraged. We look at it and think to ourselves, As long as we can encourage someone to keep going, then our job is done, but who is going to encourage us when we need it? Yes, an encourager is strong in many ways, especially when we ask God for added strength to encourage everyone. However, a weak moment will slip in from time to time, and it often goes unnoticed because we cater to everyone else. We need someone to pour us some encouraging juice once in a while.

Pray for us encouragers that we may continue to encourage you.

THEIR APPROVAL WAS NEVER NEEDED

"Everyone who believes has God's approval through faith in Jesus Christ." Romans 3:22 (God's Word [GW])

*D*on't wait for someone else's approval to live your life. It doesn't matter how close you are to someone. Waiting for their approval can cause you to delay your gift. Know that a delay could be a set up to not start something that you've already asked God to bless you with. Everyone's approval is not needed for you to go forth in life.

Know who to turn to, pray, and go for it.

SOMEONE WHO IS SOLID

"Therefore, confess your sins to
one another and pray for one
another, that you may be healed.
The prayer of a righteous
person has great power as it is
working." James 5:16 (ESV)

*M*ake sure that you have an "ol' school" friend on your team. Someone that understands where you are coming from will let you vent. Someone who never judges your slip-ups, will correct you when you are wrong. But most importantly, you both can laugh and talk about anything. That same person that will never share your conversation with the next person and will forever have your back without thinking twice. A friend that will pray with you, and when you can't find the words to say, they will pray for you.

If you have someone, hold on to them because they are not built like that anymore.

REMAIN BEING HAPPY FOR YOURSELF

"I will strengthen you, I will help
you, I will uphold you with my
righteous right hand." Isaiah
41:10 (ESV)

*D*on't let what others think about you make
you feel bad. Know who you are while you
continue to be happy. People will always have
something to say, especially when they are keeping the
focus of hiding something about themselves. It's like a
person wants others to know you from the description
they give.

Don't be moved by the mood that they try to show you. Instead, let your happy mood help them to find themselves.

PAINFUL TRANSITIONS PRODUCE POWERFUL PEOPLE

"Do not be conformed to the world,
   but be transformed by the
   renewal of your mind, that by
   testing you may discern what is
   the will of God, what is good
   and acceptable and perfect."
Romans 12:2 (ESV)

This one hits hard when we are going through that transition of pain, rejection, or taking a loss. I used to think that I had enough God in me that I could make it through anything unscathed. I wasn't perfect at all, but I thought that I was exempt because of my faith and trust in God, but a rejection had me feeling low. Then back-to-back deaths hit me hard, and the pain was unbearable. However, the transitioning showed me that I had to go through it to see how strong I was to come out of it. We have to learn how to fight back with the tools that God gave us.

My Bible and prayers were my secret weapon to produce the power that I needed to overcome what had me down.

NEVER LET YOUR IN-BETWEEN SITUATION BLOCK YOU FROM TRUSTING GOD

"Cast all your anxiety on him
    because he cares about you." 1
Peter 5:7 (NIV)

YES, GO THROUGH IT!

FIGHT THROUGH IT!

CRY THROUGH IT!

PRAY THROUGH IT!

Don't you ever stop trusting God. He's on our side waiting to bring you out.

ONE OF THE BEST FEELINGS IS WAKING UP WITH A SMILE

"Give thanks to the Lord, for he is
good; his love endures forever."
Psalm 107:1 (NIV)

I had to learn how to thank God for the little things that He has blessed me with. I don't have it all together, but just the fact that God is keeping me together is good enough for me. Just when I think about how I wake up with a smile, I am reminded that it's the simple things that we can take for granted. It's the little things that are preparing us for bigger.

At times, we must have a "Just Because" smile —

Just because God woke me up

Just because I have no pain

Just because I'm able to see a new day

Just because I'm in my right state of mind

Just because my family is accounted for

Just because I have a roof over my head

Just because I'm not where I used to be

And because of it all, I wake up with a smile.

AFTERWORD

First and foremost, I want to give thanks and praise to God for blessing me with the vision and determination to write this book.

The task of translating my thoughts onto paper was not an easy one as each page caused me to reflect on unpleasant memories of past traumas I had to endure. Despite these feelings, I found comfort in knowing that my words would be made available to help someone else in need of encouragement.

The journey of writing this book took me to places where I had to believe that I could do it when no one else thought that I could. I had to put my trust in GOD. There were many nights that I woke up with thoughts racing through my mind and I just wrote.

In closing, let me leave you with this…NEVER X OUT YOUR VISION with SOMEONE ELSE'S OPINION. You will succeed by EnCouraging Yourself to "Write the Vision and Make it plain" (Habakkuk 2:2 KJV). Because I went with what I had, wrote the vision, and made it plain to GOD, here I am Encouraging you.

ACKNOWLEDGMENTS

Only a few people knew what I was doing and I truly have been BLESSED to have these WONDERFUL people who no matter what time I called, FaceTimed, texted, or needed them to come through to lean on their shoulder, they made themselves available to listen to me. When they didn't hear from me, they checked in on my progress. They encouraged me through my discouragement and have given me feedback, not advice.

My Children, Terrance, Tyrone, and Trinnaye, are the best. My Greatest Blessings from God…Thank you for everything.

Thank You Pastor Marquis Boone. You have inspired me so much through the years. When I told you my vision, you listened, put me in contact with the right person (Danielle Butler) and now here I am. I Love you, Brody!

Danielle Butler, I feel like I've known you for years. I talked, you listened, and it was on from there. Thank you for trusting me to get it done. Thank you for your patience, your input and most of all, for making it happen for me. This is just the beginning!

Thank You Kevin Rabb (Ralo) for sticking by me 100 percent. I couldn't/wouldn't choose a better male best friend. Our in-the-middle-of-the-night talks about the book and just being there at all times. The loyalty that you have shown is outstanding. I love and appreciate you.

Thank you, Lindy Newton. Through all of my encouraging, you made sure that you poured back into me during times when I was writing this book. You have pushed me, dropped tears with me, and given me a shoulder to lay on on many occasions. Your support is dope. I love and appreciate you so much!

Thank you, Anthony Hill. You are truly a blessing on so many levels. There was a time when I didn't understand why you were going so hard on me, telling me not to lose focus and to keep writing. I understand now (Focus and Build)!

Thank you to my praying partner Tanese Lee. You didn't know that I was at this stage of writing but all it took at any time was for me to send a text saying "911", and your reply was "I'm on it" or out of nowhere you would call me and say "I felt something. What's going on?" You laughed me through months of putting this book together and didn't know anything about it. If you don't have one, PLEASE get you a praying partner!

Lastly, **thank you to my friend Rob Garris.** From Day 1 when I told you what I was doing, you gave your feedback and said "Don't talk about it. Just get it done." You supported my ideas with encouragement. You dealt with my pressure through it all, and I'm grateful for you.

ABOUT THE AUTHOR

Sharnette Berrie is the Founder of I EnCouraged Me. I EnCouraged Me is an inspirational platform that aims to encourage individuals that are experiencing various levels of personal hurt, trauma, and depression, all which Sharnette experienced firsthand.

Sharnette's ambition for creating I EnCouraged Me began when she started writing a motivational book of quotes she had been inspired to write during her struggles with mental, verbal, and physical abuse. She was looking for a way that she could encourage other women to find strength during their weakest moments. It was while writing her book that she recalled how encouraging herself helped her to overcome her inner struggles. Sharnette then shifted her focus from herself to helping others.

Currently, she has a Facebook page, "I EnCouraged Me" which is helping her vision of encouraging people from all walks of life come to fruition. Since beginning her book, Sharnette facilitated a motivational workshop to a group of women and men who are recovering from abuse. Since then, she has been encouraging people through her everyday Facebook posts and is looking forward to forming a motivational group in late 2021.

Sharnette Berrie is the eighth of eleven children born to her mother, the late Venna I. Green-Berrie. She was raised by her maternal grandmother, the late Pastor Viola Green in Fairfield County Connecticut. From a little girl, Sharnette attended her family's church, Ames Temple Church, which was founded by her late Great Grandmother, National Mother Emmaline Ames. She was an active member of the Church Choir that consisted of her sisters.

She received her AS Degree in Criminal Justice in December 2018, followed by her BA Degree in Human Services (May 2020) from Post University.

Sharnette has three children whom she calls her "3Ts": Terrance, Tyrone (Ashley) and Trinnaye as well as three grands - Gianna, Lana and Jayden.

Sharnette was brought up on the saying, "If I can help someone along the way, then my living will not be in vain." She has adopted this as her motto and life mission.

CPSIA information can be obtained
at www.ICGtesting.com
Printed in the USA
BVHW031932121221
623864BV00005B/165